theatre & violence

Theatre&
Series Standing Order: ISBN 978–0–230–20327–3

You can receive future titles in this series as they are published by placing a standing order. Please contact your bookseller or, in case of difficulty, write to us at the address below with your name and address, the title of the series and the ISBN quoted above.

Customer Services Department, Macmillan Distribution Ltd, Houndmills, Basingstoke, Hampshire, RG21 6XS, UK

theatre &
violence

Lucy Nevitt

palgrave
macmillan

First published 2013 by
PALGRAVE MACMILLAN

Palgrave Macmillan in the UK is an imprint of Macmillan Publishers Limited, registered in England, company number 785998, of Houndmills, Basingstoke, Hampshire RG21 6XS.

Palgrave Macmillan in the US is a division of St Martin's Press LLC, 175 Fifth Avenue, New York, NY 10010.

Palgrave Macmillan is the global academic imprint of the above companies and has companies and representatives throughout the world.

Palgrave® and Macmillan® are registered trademarks in the United States, the United Kingdom, Europe and other countries

ISBN: 978–1–137–30227–4 paperback

This book is printed on paper suitable for recycling and made from fully managed and sustained forest sources. Logging, pulping and manufacturing processes are expected to conform to the environmental regulations of the country of origin.

A catalogue record for this book is available from the British Library.

A catalog record for this book is available from the Library of Congress.

contents

Contents

series editors' preface

The theatre is everywhere, from entertainment districts to the fringes, from the rituals of government to the ceremony of the courtroom, from the spectacle of the sporting arena to the theatres of war. Across these many forms stretches a theatrical continuum through which cultures both assert and question themselves.

Theatre has been around for thousands of years, and the ways we study it have changed decisively. It's no longer enough to limit our attention to the canon of Western dramatic literature. Theatre has taken its place within a broad spectrum of performance, connecting it with the wider forces of ritual and revolt that thread through so many spheres of human culture. In turn, this has helped make connections across disciplines; over the past fifty years, theatre and performance have been deployed as key metaphors and practices with which to rethink gender, economics, war, language, the fine arts, culture and one's sense of self.

Theatre & is a long series of short books which hopes to capture the restless interdisciplinary energy of theatre and performance. Each book explores connections between theatre and some aspect of the wider world, asking how the theatre might illuminate the world and how the world might illuminate the theatre. Each book is written by a leading theatre scholar and represents the cutting edge of critical thinking in the discipline.

We have been mindful, however, that the philosophical and theoretical complexity of much contemporary academic writing can act as a barrier to a wider readership. A key aim for these books is that they should all be readable in one sitting by anyone with a curiosity about the subject. The books are challenging, pugnacious, visionary sometimes and, above all, clear. We hope you enjoy them.

Jen Harvie and Dan Rebellato

foreword

My most intense experience with violence in the thea-tre took place in the 1990s in Sarah Kane's play *Phaedra's Love*, at a time when she, Mark Ravenhill *et al.* were confronting audiences with some very uncomfortable viewing.

I think it's almost impossible to pull off a convincing act of violence (or sex for that matter) onstage. I have seen/learned carefully choreographed fights, and that's exactly how they end up looking. And suspension of disbelief just doesn't stretch to accepting that an actor is really hurting his colleague.

But I do remember being blown away by *Woyzeck* at the Gate Theatre in 1997, directed by Sarah Kane, when Michael Shannon, the very intense American actor in the title role, threw himself around with such abandon he ended the play bleeding. From my own experience of having been directed by Sarah the previous year in *Phaedra's Love*, I imagine she probably didn't ask it of him, but neither would she have discouraged it.

I seem to remember Sarah telling me that *Phaedra's Love* (also at the Gate) was her comedy, after the furore surrounding *Blasted*. I suppose it's not surprising that there was a lot of laughter involved in trying to decide how best to credibly cut off and barbeque a man's genitals. The embarrassment factor combined with an effort to offset the visceral nastiness we were trying to achieve.

When it came to 'special effects', youth and bolshieness abounded, and it was fun to think about shocking any establishment theatregoers who might come our way. However, remember that throwing pretend viscera around can bring a hefty dry-cleaning bill when they happen to hit a casting director.

I know Sarah delighted in giving directors 'impossible' stage directions, and, in her uncompromising take on a classic by Seneca, she gave herself plenty of headaches. No messenger delivering news of horrors happening elsewhere. A blowjob, rape, murder and evisceration for all to see. Just as she had shown the violence of an imploding Bosnia land in a Leeds hotel room.

It's important to say that Sarah made rehearsals a lot of fun, as well as intense – surprising and naughty. They gave scope for her capacity for mischief. I remember her locking me and Cas Harkins (Hippolytus) in a basement room of the rehearsal space for a bit of a sense memory exercise (I was young and up for it!) while she (I later learned) was having pizza with a mate. And an exercise to bring about the need to speak involved stuffing socks in my mouth. They were clean socks.

I do not mean to make light of the violent acts portrayed onstage; I just think, led by Sarah, we all felt the hypocrisy of how violence was being reported in our society. At arm's length, in the paper in salacious detail, on canvas — these were acceptable. But right in front of them onstage, with authenticity, seemed to upset people in a variety of ways.

Recently, I've had to cut off someone's head in Howard Barker's *Judith: A Parting from the Body*, in a *very* small space. It was all about the angles, but I believe it was quite effective. To make the sound of the last bit of detaching, one of the actors sawed in and out of a sandbag. I think it helped a lot. It's all in the detail.

In Edward Bond's *Bingo* (it's no surprise that these amazing writers come to mind), a young woman is gibbeted. Michelle Tate stood completely still as the dead girl high up on the gibbet for 20 minutes. It was incredibly disturbing. And occasionally irritating, when audience members thought she was a dummy.

One of the most horrifying moments of violence I ever saw onstage (it's subjective, of course) was in *The Beauty Queen of Leenane*. You believed you had seen a pan of water come to the boil on a stove. And this boiling water was then thrown over someone. It was very much how the actor (Jane Brennan) chose to do it. Not in a sudden violent way, but matter-of-factly.

I also very much enjoyed the National Theatre of Scotland production of *Black Watch*, directed by John Tiffany, in which testosterone-fuelled violence was conveyed through movement, almost dance.

There are all sorts of violence. I worked with my husband in a play by Leo Butler, *The Early Bird*. The play centres on a married couple whose child has gone missing. Our director and designer came up with a Perspex box in which we were enclosed for the entire play, with the audience completely surrounding us. Animals in a zoo, a TV freakshow, or the inside of a crumbling obsessing mind. The characters proceed to torture themselves and each other psychologically about their daughter's fate. We tried and failed in our efforts not to take it home!

So, I've probably concentrated on violence in a very literal way. Of course, so much violence in theatre is in the words. Sarah's work, Bond and Pinter are prime examples.

It seems to me that drama always had to reflect the violent forging of our world. And the refinement and changes in presentation of that violence in theatre continue to keep pace with the kinds of violence we inflict upon one another. Whether it's subtle struggles within a family, dressed-up corporate violence, or state-funded annihilation.

Catherine Cusack is a London-based actor. She started working, mostly onstage, twenty-six years ago. She recently performed in Bingo *by Edward Bond at the Young Vic Theatre and in* All That Fall, *Samuel Beckett's radio play performed in London, starring Michael Gambon and Eileen Atkins.*

theatre & violence

Two examples of spectating violence

Example One. The stage set represents a hotel room that has been blown up by a mortar bomb. In the debris lie two characters, a soldier and the man he has just raped. We have been shown the rape, during which the soldier was 'crying his heart out'. We also witnessed the man engaging in his own acts of violence and sexual violence against a young woman, both before and after the explosion that destroyed the room. The soldier grips the man's head in his hands. He puts his mouth over one of the man's eyes, sucks it out, bites it off and eats it. He does the same to the other eye.

Example Two. The television shows the opening credits of a news programme. Across the bottom of the screen we read the banner 'Breaking

News'. Above this we are shown a series of filmed images, all from the same event but cut together so that time is truncated. A skyscraper collapses into rubble; a second tower beside it remains standing. People run and scream; there is chaos on the ground. An aircraft flies towards the second tower, then crashes into it. Bodies fall from high windows. There is dust and rubble and frantic but largely aimless movement. A reporter shouts into a microphone.

What are the differences between these two depictions of violence, and between the two acts of spectatorship being undertaken by the people who watch them? It is true but simplistic to say that one is real and the other, not. The images of violence performed in the context of a play (the first example was from Sarah Kane's *Blasted* (Royal Court Theatre Upstairs, London, 1995)) may have effects on its audience that are very real, and that linger long after the spectators and actors have left the theatre. On the other hand, one of the most common responses among witnesses to the 9/11 attack on the World Trade Center in New York was that it was like a movie.

This is a book about theatre, performance and violence, and as such it is inescapably fascinated with the idea of reality. Simulated violence, in which the violence and its physical effects are illusory and no bodily harm is done, is connected with reality in so many ways that it quickly becomes impossible to assign it a simple definition of 'not real'. Actual violence, when the harm is happening as it appears to be, is such a common feature of the news that many people have developed a spectatorial distance from it. We know it is real, but paradoxically its impact can be less immediate and strong, and less long-lasting and troubling, than the impact of some simulated violence presented in theatres.

Simulation and actuality are preoccupations of this study and I will explore the many ways in which they can interact and inform different representations of violence, from fights in plays to battle re-enactments and professional wrestling shows, from body art to hunger strikes and acts of war. The other conceptual through-line is spectatorship: the experience of being in the position of 'audience' for acts of simulated or actual violence.

In 2007 the feminist political philosopher Adriana Cavarero published a book that responded to acts of actual violence that are usually described as 'terrorism'. Her argument is partly driven by an analysis of the effects of these acts, not only on the victims who suffer their immediate physical effects of death and mutilation but also on those who witness them. It is in effect an analysis of spectatorship, and the book is called *Horrorism*.

Cavarero begins by going back to the etymological roots of the word *terror* and its equivalents in various languages, which all connect with a physical experience of fear: importantly, the desire to flee and the bodily movement towards flight. With this interpretation of *terror* she contrasts *horror*, a word whose etymology links it to the sensation of being frozen. While *terror* is linked to action – individual flight or mass panic – *horror* connotes paralysis, stasis, the response of helplessly doing nothing. Cavarero suggests that *horrorism* would be a more appropriate term for describing attacks on the helpless, and also for describing acts of violence that provoke responses of helpless stasis.

Without going into the details of the fascinating discussion that she builds from this starting point, it is clear that Cavarero's linguistic argument should resonate strongly with scholars of performance. Does theatre generate horror more frequently than terror? What might we learn from experiencing spectatorial horror in a theatre, where it can be pleasurable as well as disturbing? Cavarero's term prompts us to put spectatorial experience to the fore in our considerations of theatre and violence. It also insists that we notice the workings of language, and the significance of the choices that we make when assigning words to actions, images, representations and their effects.

Thinking about theatre and violence

Violence often seems to be everywhere. It's hard not to be constantly aware of acts of violence in the world, while a sense of threat from possible violence, large-scale or individual, is something most people have lived with from a fairly early age. Violence is also, as a subject, enormous. We can't talk about 'violence' for long without needing to apply categories, and there are many different directions from which the subject can be viewed.

We can classify violence as physical, verbal, psychological, emotional, intellectual or spiritual. We can categorise it by scale: from a fight between two people to a battle or war. Violence can be considered from the perspective of its cause (what motivates it), its form or its effects. We can think about the way that it is contextualised or regulated. The length of time over which violence between the same people or groups occurs sometimes helps us understand its context: whether abuse is prolonged, ongoing or repeated, for example. Legal systems usually recognise that intention is important, and proof of accident or self-defence can sometimes mitigate a charge of murder.

It can also be useful to consider the different means by which violence is enacted. We might perceive a distinction between an attack launched from a distance and an encounter in which those involved can see one another, or look into each other's eyes. We might respond differently to unarmed combat (body-to-body contact using hands, feet, teeth, heads and so on) than we would to the use of blades, or projectiles such as arrows, or bullets. Some people feel that there is a moral or ethical difference between violence involving only men and violence against, by or between women and/or children; that from men, for example, violence might be more acceptable, understandable or even 'natural'.

So why theatre and violence? What are the reasons for linking these two ideas together in a book? There are two ways of addressing this question. First, does thinking about *violence* matter? If so, is theatre a good place to think about it? Second, why does thinking about the *performance* of violence matter?

Thinking about violence

Thinking about violence matters because of its ubiquity, because of the terror and pain it causes, because it is, in its actual forms in the world, bad. In general terms violence has a relationship to power and powerlessness. In specific examples it has effects that include pain and death, trauma, fear and escalations of further violence. The process of conceptualising violence requires both theoretical abstraction and empathetic imagination. Violence is basic and ordinary (for many people it is, in different ways and contexts, normal) and yet profoundly unpleasant to think about, all at once.

Theatre permits and enables us to contemplate violence. A piece of theatre is a collaborative act of imagination in which theatre-makers and their audiences can explore possibilities and fantasies as well as reconsidering known realities. In the theatre we can play out different imaginary versions of the world, and so theatre provides space, structures and contexts for the contemplation of actual and potential violence. Theatre plays with cause and effect and with sophisticated analyses of concepts and events. Since fictional framing and the relative safety of the not-real enable theatre-makers to push their ideas to the extremes of cultural imagination, it is inevitable that theatre will be concerned with violence.

Philip Ridley's play *Mercury Fur* (Drum Theatre, Plymouth, UK, 2005) is set in London in an imagined future in which the children who are the central characters distribute drugs (hallucinogenic butterflies) and arrange private 'parties' in order to survive. These parties involve the enactment of the violent sexual fantasy of a single 'guest'; child victims are provided by other children to be tortured, raped and killed by paying adults. The play contains sequences of extreme violence. The drugged ten-year-old victim, known only as Party Piece, is tortured onstage. The brutal fantasy enactment itself, which has been discussed enough in advance for the audience to know what it involves, takes place offstage but is communicated vividly and horrifically through an extended sequence of sound.

The circumstances of the play are imagined and they are extreme; it is a disturbing play for its audience to witness. Yet this play is the imagined extension of aspects that the playwright sees in our existing culture. In a 2009 interview published in the journal *New Theatre Quarterly* Ridley connects the subject matter of *Mercury Fur* with his perception of the increasing levels of interest in (and availability of) violent pornography, representing the events in the play as 'the logical conclusion' of this already-present industry (p. 115). A central theme of *Mercury Fur* is the breakdown of memory and identity under the combined influence of brutality and drugs. The play's violence is narratively associated with the effects of the butterflies, which have been introduced by an invading power to subdue and control the populace. In the same interview Ridley links this idea to recent and current events, identifying the destruction of a people's history as 'stage one of an invasion for any imperialist force' (p. 115).

In her 2006 play *Lemkin's House* (78th Street Theatre Lab, New York), Catherine Filloux imagines the real historical figure Raphael Lemkin trapped in an afterlife that takes

7

the form of a dilapidated house. Lemkin, the lawyer who coined the term *genocide* and fought to have genocide recognised as a crime in international law, is haunted throughout the play by atrocities that have happened since the adoption of the United Nations Convention on the Prevention and Punishment of the Crime of Genocide in 1948. He, and through him the audience, encounters horrific violence and appalling suffering, but since he is dead and unable to leave the house in which he finds himself, he is powerless to intervene.

The central character's helplessness here represents and explores the feelings that many of the audience might experience when learning about distant atrocities. Filloux's play does not offer an immediate solution to this helplessness — after all, there is no simple way for an individual to intervene in situations of genocide. It does provide us with the opportunity to acknowledge the horror of such events and to notice and respond in turn to our own responses to that horror. As autonomous individuals, what we do with that process is up to us. The theatre provides us with an experience, for many reasons perhaps an experience of greater immediacy than a reported news story, on which we can reflect and to which we can, if we choose, seek out ways to respond.

This book is written from the perspective that it is necessary and desirable to use theatre and performance to help us to contemplate violence. When violence happens elsewhere, at a distance, not to me or anyone of my acquaintance, it is easy for me to know about it without contemplating it.

Images and descriptions of violence abound hour after hour on the news media. Twenty-four-hour news is by its nature ever-present; there is no special space or time in which audiences can pause to think about this knowledge of violence, violence's reality and its implications. Theatre, whether it directly represents real-world examples or employs fiction and fantasy to explore violent possibilities, provides us with space, focus and stimuli for a concentrated consideration of the subject.

Thinking about the performance of violence

Of course, performance is not a single, stable entity, and so it is also necessary and important to think about the ways that violence can be performed. When we think about the *performance of violence* it soon becomes clear that here is a topic on which almost everyone has an opinion. Performed violence can prompt responses of extraordinary passion and fury in people who are quite removed from the theatre and its audiences.

In 1965 even people who had never been to the theatre had heard or read about Edward Bond's play *Saved* (Royal Court Theatre, London). Or rather, they knew about one series of actions in one of its scenes: the stoning to death of a baby in its pram. In 1982 theatre director Michael Bogdanov faced criminal charges at the Old Bailey because of one sequence in Howard Brenton's *The Romans in Britain* (National Theatre, London, 1980) – the performed anal rape that left the play indelibly associated with accusations of shocking violence and, as the charges expressed it, 'gross indecency between two actors'. In 1995 Sarah Kane's *Blasted* became notorious for what was represented in the media as gratuitous and disgusting violence, coming in for an extra share of vitriol because Kane was a young, female playwright.

In all of these examples, reviews of the productions listed the violent acts that were performed as though they were the ingredients of the play. It seems that performed violence has the potential to overpower the context in which it is shown. The observation or the naming of violence can overshadow spectatorial responses. It can even obscure the play as a whole, positioning that play in the canon of theatre history as controversial: 'a violent play'.

This last phrase is a particularly interesting use of language. Violence in theatre crosses boundaries of period, genre and context. Many plays and performances depict or describe violence, but not all of them are thought of as violent plays. The phrase 'a violent play' suggests on one level that the play itself is an act of violence. (This idea that showing can also be doing is explored in more detail later in this book, in the section on performativity and ideology.) Another familiar idea is that violence in performance might be 'gratuitous' or 'unnecessary'. These too are interesting words, because they unintentionally imply the existence of their conceptual opposite, 'necessary' or 'useful' performances of violence.

In *Lemkin's House*, Lemkin meets Jack, a 'natty UN official' who is monitoring the slaughter in Rwanda of Tutsi people by Hutus, and learns that politicians since 1948 have frequently responded to the official recognition of genocide as a crime by simply avoiding the term:

Jack:	We don't use 'the G word'.
Lemkin:	The G word?
Jack:	It hasn't escalated to that level. We aren't allowed to use that word.
Lemkin:	Dismemberment of Tutsis, Tutsi women's sex organs hanging from trees is not sufficient escalation for you?
Jack:	The word makes certain security council members nervous. (p. 27)

Lemkin's incredulous response a few lines later – 'There are actually leaders who think if they don't use a word, they don't have to do anything about it?' – may well echo thoughts that spectators have had outside the theatre in response to discussions of this issue in the news. It also offers us a way of thinking about the possible usefulness of portraying violent action onstage. Violence exists in the world as reality and potential. The choice not to represent it will not make it go away, and certainly shouldn't mean that we don't have to do anything about it. Theatre and other performance contexts *do* offer the possibility for useful and necessary considerations of violence.

It is not possible to make judgements about or develop an analysis of 'violence in performance' as if this were a single phenomenon. We must always consider the ways in which acts of violence are positioned within the wider frame of the play or performance in which they occur. We must also consider the ways in which they are depicted and performed, which means that analysis of moments in performance (the choices made by fight directors, directors, performers and designers, as well as the expectations and experiences of spectators) is just as important as the analysis of any written script.

This book offers a number of conceptual approaches to thinking about performance and violence. The next section explores spectatorship and style, looking at the different ways in which audiences might experience a performance of violence and the ways in which theatrical convention can influence those spectatorial encounters. The section on causality addresses ideas about the effect on spectators of watching simulated violence, and the following sections on performativity and ideology and on the canon offer different ways of thinking about 'effect'. Actuality and simulation are concepts that run through the book, but they are addressed directly in a discussion of stage combat, gaming and violent body art, before the argument moves on to consider the framing, witnessing and theorising of actual violence, including a return to my opening example of 'terrorism' and the 9/11 attacks. The book concludes with a look at some of the many ways in which theatre and performance have been created in direct response to situations of war and political violence in recent decades.

Spectatorship

The experience of theatre is not simply individual and imaginary but also social and corporeal. Maurice Level's one-act play *Le Baiser dans la nuit* (originally performed in 1912; translated and adapted into English as *The Final Kiss* by Richard J. Hand and Michael Wilson, 2002) was written for the Grand-Guignol, a Parisian theatre celebrated and notorious for its sensational representations of violence and often erotically charged horror. Before the play begins, its central character, Henri, has been attacked with vitriol (sulphuric acid) by his former fiancée, Jeanne. Henri's face is covered during the majority of the play, and the appalling extent of his injuries is established through verbal description. In the last moments of the play Henri pours acid onto Jeanne's face in full view of the audience before removing his bandages to reveal his own ravaged face as she crawls on the floor, screaming in agony.

Structurally, *The Final Kiss* is a slow build towards a climactic moment of violent action and visual horror. The spectators who saw *Le Baiser dans la nuit* at the Grand-Guignol came in anticipation of enjoying depictions of horrific violence. There is suspense, but not from wondering whether an attack will happen: the questions are when, how and to whom the inevitable violence will occur. The spectatorial response that was expected and set up by this play was one of delighted horror; audience members were invited to relish the experience of being terrified and disgusted by the performed action onstage.

In their book *Grand-Guignol: The French Theatre of Horror* (2002), Hand and Wilson offer a detailed analysis of the Grand-Guignol, its plays and its audiences. In connection with their discussion of spectatorship, they quote Philip Brophy on cinema:

> The contemporary horror film *knows* that you've seen it before; it *knows* that you know what is about to happen; and it knows that you know it knows you know. And none of it means a thing, as the cheapest trick in the book will still tense your muscles, quicken your heart and jangle your nerves. (p. 70; emphasis in original)

Hand and Wilson also cite David Cronenberg, who 'writes that "the appeal of horror is beyond politics" and argues that, although it can be *eventually* interpreted politically, its appeal is "right into the viscera, before it gets to the brain"' (p. 71).

We know that action can be communicated and understood intellectually. When one character hits another with a forceful punch to the stomach, spectators go through a mental process of analysing and understanding that image. The force of the punch equates to a probable level of pain, which spectators might calculate in relation to the relative size and apparent strength of aggressor and victim. A punch to the stomach can cause loss of breath, and spectators might look for evidence of the victim being winded in this way. They might expect him to double over and perhaps stagger back a few steps before regaining his balance. If he does so, the punch has had the expected effect. If he does not, or if he falls completely to the floor, spectators might adjust their understanding of aggressor, victim or both. In other words the punch will be read in relation to the action of the aggressor and the responses of the victim. Members of an audience engage in a detailed intellectual analysis of shifting meanings as they are presented. And they do this very quickly, as the action unfolds.

At the same time, spectators are having a physical experience. We understand physical contact partly because we have experienced it in our own bodies. Even if you have never been punched in the stomach, you can imagine its effect because your ongoing experience of your body frames your understanding of the world. You know what pain is because you have felt it. This can affect the way that you experience performed violence as a spectator. A convincingly performed stomach punch might cause you to flinch, or to gasp ever so slightly for breath. As you follow a fast and furious sword fight, your heart rate might increase a little and you might experience a surge of adrenaline. Perhaps you have been in the audience when an image was shown (or even the act described) of a man being kneed or kicked in the groin. How many of those present winced or crossed their legs or moved their hands protectively towards their own groins?

Some forms of performance deliberately explore what happens to the presentation and reception of violence when the audience knows that the acts being performed are causing actual bodily pain or wounds to the performers. These circumstances change the nature of the spectatorial experience and will be discussed in a later section. In the majority of cases, however, spectators know that what they are witnessing is simulation and not violence, and this must also contextualise (and sometimes complicate) the experience.

A performed act of violence rarely, if ever, generates a single response. A spectator can be simultaneously engrossed in fiction and aware of simulation; a spectacle of violence can be enjoyable and sickening at the same time. Much performed violence deliberately provokes a confusion of responses in its audience. When we analyse violence in plays and performances, it is important not to overlook the complexities of intention and reception. Every moment in a performance is made up of a series of precise choices with far-reaching implications. We have seen how the way in which the 'idea' of a punch is turned into action can determine the meanings it communicates. It is also helpful to recognise the importance of theatrical convention to the process of communicating ideas in performance.

Stylistic choices and conventions

For example, comic violence is usually characterised by having no lasting effect on, or causing no lasting pain to, its victim. In slapstick, one form of comic violence, the relationship between cause and effect is often humorously distorted. Perhaps a character will be on the receiving end of enormous punches but continue to get up for more – think about the violence in cartoons, where the impact is immediate and huge but short-lived. Slapstick sometimes also distorts the relationship between action and reaction:

a tiny push sends someone flying across the stage or a giant punch elicits no response at all. There is a contract with the audience here: we can laugh because there are no consequences and therefore no need for empathy or analysis. It has been agreed through the conventions of the genre that these characters do not experience pain and injury in the way that we would.

It is not always straightforward to divorce comic violence from its implications. In a way that is difficult to explain, much of the comedy of Punch and Judy puppet shows comes from Mr Punch beating Judy repeatedly with a cudgel. For some spectators and critics, however, the associations between this comic image of wife-beating and actual domestic abuse are too strong and too close for detachment to be possible. In cases such as this the convention and therefore the comedy might fail because a spectator is unable or unwilling to accept a separation of the performed actions from their implications.

A different example of violence in comedy can be found in Act Two of Noël Coward's *Private Lives* (Phoenix Theatre, London, 1930). Divorced couple Elyot and Amanda have run away together. Because they keep quarrelling, they have established a rule: if things start to get nasty, one of them will say 'sollocks' and they must then let two minutes pass without speaking. This works twice, and structures the act into a pattern: loving conversation descends into irritation; the code word perpetuates a long silence and a return to loving conversation. While this is funny in itself, the comic payoff comes on the third time through. The couple have begun to argue about a gramophone record. Elyot sees the danger:

> Elyot (*suddenly stricken with remorse*):　Amanda darling – Sollocks.
> Amanda (*furiously*):　Sollocks yourself. (*She breaks the record over his head*)

Elyot slaps Amanda's face, she hits him back, and the fight escalates physically as they scream abuse at one another and struggle violently on the floor, knocking over most of the furniture. Coward's stage direction details the fight, move by move, with great precision (pp. 62–64).

It is obvious that exaggerated slapstick violence is not what Coward intended for this scene, which tends to be funniest when the fight is played as roughly and scrappily as possible. The comedy here comes not from the style of the fight but from its context: the incongruity of these upper-class, highly decorous characters abandoning all rules of social behaviour to descend into a physical, furniture-breaking brawl.

Acts of violence can be performed in different styles, and, perhaps surprisingly, the question of whether they are *realistic* is not a particularly helpful way of approaching stylistic choice. Performed fights rarely show what would happen if the depicted situation were actually occurring. This is partly because of the need for actions to be visible and legible to an audience. The action that would be most likely in an actual encounter might not be sufficiently large, clear or interesting to communicate from a stage, so choreographic choices are often based more on readability than on likelihood.

Furthermore, it is not always easy for a spectator with little personal experience of fighting or violence to judge what is realistic and what is not. This is particularly the case when weapons and/or skilled fighting are involved, because the untrained audience member lacks the knowledge to assess the authenticity of the performed fight. Indeed, many people get their understanding of what a fight looks and sounds like from film, television, computer games and theatre, creating a cycle of expectation that has more to do with performance conventions and traditions than reality.

Realism is a theatrical convention like any other, available as an option to performers and directors. Stylistic choices are motivated by desired effect, which is influenced by many factors. In Bond's *Saved*, the sequence in which the young men kill the baby functions as both metaphor and social commentary. Violence explores a political idea, connected to the playwright's views on the inequities of capitalism. In his 1977 essay 'On Violence' Bond argues that:

> the causes of human violence can be easily summed up. It occurs in situations of injustice. It is caused not only by physical threats, but even more significantly by threats to human dignity. [...] [W]henever there is serious and constant

> violence, that is a sign of the presence of some
> major social injustice. (p. 13)

The murder of the baby is proof of the social injustice under which the young men's lives are lived. That it is a baby they kill suggests the 'persecution of victims by victims' that Bond identifies as resulting from the powerlessness of the oppressed to alter their intolerable situation (p. 15). There is also a strong metaphor here, as the baby's death can be interpreted as the destruction of potential, the abandonment of interest in the future.

With these political points in mind it is clear that this particular violent sequence should be performed according to conventions that communicate actual behaviour. Other plays seem to offer a freer range of interpretive choices. In Shakespeare's *Titus Andronicus*, a play filled with violence and gore, Titus's daughter Lavinia is raped by two men. They cut off her tongue and her hands to prevent her from communicating their identities. Unlike most of the violence in this play, the rape and dismemberment take place off-stage, but when Lavinia enters the audience is shown the effects of the violence on her body. For performers and directors there is a clear choice here: how should these effects be represented?

A number of directors, perhaps most famously Peter Brook at Stratford's Shakespeare Memorial Theatre in 1955, have chosen forms of symbolic stylisation, deliberately moving away from convincing blood and performed pain in favour of a compelling stage image. Martin White's

1998 book *Renaissance Drama in Action* offers an analytical case study of this moment in performance. White quotes Richard David's precise description of Brook's production:

> Vivien Leigh, as Lavinia, entered with her 'right arm outstretched and head drooping away from it, left arm crooked with the wrist at her mouth', her hair 'in disorder over face and shoulders' and 'scarlet streamers, symbols of her mutilation' trailing from wrists and mouth. [...] 'a small stylized tune was played on harp harmonics followed by piano' which produced 'an eloquent, not a horrific moment'. (p. 190)

The effect is beautiful as well as appalling. It foregrounds the spectator's sympathy for Lavinia's plight. She is an innocent victim, and the spectator is guided to contemplate her suffering without being asked to imagine too precisely its actual manifestation on her body. The concept of suffering is here abstracted from its physical implications of pain and mess. It is a powerful image that stays in the mind, signifying the horror of violation and allowing the spectator to respond entirely emotionally. It is an image designed to make us cry but not to make us sick. Constructed as an image, it is intended to fix our eyes on the stage and hold us powerfully within the moment. As we watch Leigh's entrance, our absorption in Lavinia's suffering makes us forget our own bodies. It does not occur to us to look away.

Theatrical stylisation of this kind can be captivating. The image remains long after the performance is over precisely because of its contrast between aesthetic beauty and the horror of the actions whose effects it depicts. People who saw this production onstage more than fifty years ago can still describe it, and the horrified sense that it gave them of the enormity of the character's suffering. And this is a crucial point: Brook's choice was to communicate *suffering*. The image communicates very little about brutal violence and rape.

In contrast, other productions have emphasised the bodily aspects of what has been done to Lavinia, some using sensationalist tactics to provoke a physical response from those watching. White quotes a description of a production in South Africa in 1970:

> In one scene the twice ravished Lavinia staggers on to the stage with her hands severed and her tongue cut out. Pointing her bleeding stumps at the audience she tries to speak, but blood froths from her mouth. Behind me a young man groaned, and clutching his stomach, rushed out of the theatre. (p. 191)

This time the image is sickening and it forces those watching to notice their own physical responses. This staging wants to make you feel sick before it makes you cry, and it utilises theatrical techniques to achieve this end. The surprise of the frothing-blood-from-the-mouth effect and the direct acknowledgement of the audience when Lavinia's bleeding handless wrists are displayed outwards are strategies designed to deny spectators the distance and abstraction offered by Brook's contemplation of suffering. Other productions eschew shock tactics but still explore ways in which the presentation of Lavinia's violated body can force spectators to contemplate, physically as well as emotionally, the full corporeal implications of her rape and mutilation.

It is clear from these examples that production decisions about how violence and its effects will be represented offer a judgement about that violence. It makes a difference whether we are guided towards abstracted contemplation of suffering and victimhood or pushed to respond to specific wounds on specific bodies through an imaginative process that connects what we see onstage with our sense of our own bodies. It makes a difference whether the image is beautiful or ugly. These choices are both aesthetic and political, and it is important to be fully aware of their implications.

Cause and effect

Performed representations of violence are a focus of concern for many people. Violence in films, television shows, video games and (less frequently) plays is seen by some to be a problem. Others see it as an indication of problems elsewhere. The most familiar debates about this subject centre on the possible relationships between simulated and actual violence: violence in performance and violence in the world.

Many studies over the past half-century have attempted to prove or disprove the theory that watching or engaging with simulated violence makes people more likely to behave in actually violent ways. This idea has a lot of currency, so it seems necessary to address it, and some of the ways it has been challenged and complicated, at this point in the discussion. It is important to note, however, that the cause-and-effect debate (the 'media effects model' as it is sometimes called) is more common in discussions of media violence than theatre violence.

The media effects model relies on circumstantial evidence: on correlation rather than provable connections. We can see that there is a great deal of violence in the world; we can also see that images of violence in entertainment media proliferate. It is easy – and not necessarily always wrong – to assume a connection between the two. This connection is reinforced by occasional incidents such as copycat killings or school shootings by teenagers whose interest in violent films or games is retrospectively taken as evidence that their actions were influenced by the entertainment they enjoyed.

It is also easy to refute, or at least to complicate, this argument. Correlation does not establish causality in one specific direction. Did watching simulated violence make the individuals more likely to behave violently, or were they drawn to violent media because they were also drawn to violence for other reasons? Clearly it is foolish to assert a connection between two aspects of behaviour without considering all the other things that might have contributed to the circumstances of the violent act. Because causality is essentially a linear model of thinking ('this leads to that'), many discussions of this topic fail to address the complexity of the questions being asked.

Context is also important: we must consider the way in which performed violence is framed within the representation, by narrative or other means. Some critics find fictional violence more troubling if it is enacted by positively framed characters rather than by villains who are ultimately punished. One response to this perspective is to say that when violence is the means for punishing violent villains and ensuring the restoration of 'good', the message seems to be that violence is the only, or the best, response to situations of conflict. The possibility of non-violent approaches goes unacknowledged. Of course, having people sit down to resolve their differences through discussion wouldn't offer the same visceral excitement that is offered by an action movie – spectatorial experience is always an important consideration when we are thinking about why and how people engage with violent entertainment.

A slightly more nuanced version of the causal argument focuses on the idea of violence being glamorised through the style and context of its presentation. Perhaps spectators are more likely to mimic or accept behaviours that are depicted as cool or connected with sexual attractiveness or fame. Oliver Stone's 1994 film *Natural Born Killers* explored this idea through fiction, and later became notoriously associated with it in reality when it was cited as the cause of a range of murderous attacks by young people, including the Columbine High School massacre in 1999.

Other perspectives come from arguments about *desensitisation* and *normalisation*, which suggest that ongoing exposure to images of violence gradually accustoms people to increasing degrees of violent behaviour. The idea here is that the more we see, the more we get used to seeing and the more, therefore, we are able or likely to accept: violence gets less shocking as it becomes more commonplace. These arguments are more convincing to many people, but they have their own weaknesses and have been challenged on the grounds that spectators understand context. Simulated fictional violence is understood as such and enjoyed as entertainment by people who would be horrified by actual manifestations of violence in the world.

It is important not to over-simplify the role of fictional and fantasy violence in our understanding of the world. Gerard Jones, in his 2002 book *Killing Monsters: Why Children Need Fantasy, Super Heroes, and Make-Believe Violence*, cites the example of a sixth-grade child in the USA who developed a sudden intense interest in violent films, television and video games immediately after the Columbine school murders:

> He'd heard [*Natural Born Killers*] named as a possible inspiration to more than one school shooting and he was intent on seeing it. 'That kind of, like, made it real,' he said. 'Then I got kind of used to it.' I asked him what happened then. He shrugged. 'Then I stopped thinking about it so much.' (p. 99)

Jones argues that fantasy violence can operate as a coping mechanism, controlling the fear generated by knowing about actual violence: 'When [the child] "made it real," he was taking away some of the power it held over his imagination' (p. 100).

Jones does not directly connect the power of this fear back to simulated representations, but this is an important point raised by David Trend in his 2007 discussion of *The Myth of Media Violence*:

> Media violence may not provoke people to become aggressive or commit crimes, but it does something more damaging. Media violence convinces people that they live in a violent world and that violence is required to make the world safer. [...] This anxious worldview is the result of a culture of violence that forges our core identities in fear. (p. 58)

Trend uses the desensitisation argument in an interesting way. Similarly to Jones, he believes that people 'learn about the world and form their understandings of it to a great extent from public culture' (p. 71). But Trend sees this as more of a political issue; its effect is to fix people in particular power relationships and reiterate a sense that the way things are is the only or 'natural' way for things to be. He argues that:

> The problem isn't that we have too much violence in movies and TV. The problem is that

the kind of violence portrayed is so limited.
[...] We get violent media of a very particular
kind – anesthetized to maximize its accessibil-
ity and its capacity to stimulate viewers – and
endlessly repeated stories of male strength and
good old fashioned American power. [...] The
reduction of the nation's media discourse to
a redundant series of violent spectacles does
something much worse than teaching people
to become aggressive. It teaches them to do
nothing. (p. 70)

The act of showing: performativity and ideology

One of the main problems with causal arguments is that
they engage first and foremost with what the performance
in question *shows*, rather than with what that portrayal *does*,
in a broader social sense. The importance of recognising
the context in which violent acts are represented goes further than considerations of narrative. When we consider the
possible 'effect' of simulated violence, we need to recognise
the ways in which performance is inextricably connected
with the world in which it takes place.

Directly causal arguments tend to do this too simplis-
tically, suggesting a single linear communication between
performance and spectator and assuming that the potential impact of the performance is associated solely with the
act being shown. It is easiest to imagine that the spectator
watching an act of simulated violence might be offended or

disgusted or negatively influenced by the violence itself. It is less obvious to contemplate the ways in which that portrayal of violence might do or be indicative of other things, which could in themselves have either negative or positive effects.

My point here is that simulations of violence embody certain norms, and these are not necessarily norms of violent behaviour. Violence tells us things about the culture that produced it: the kinds of power relationship on which it is built, the attitudes and values that it takes for granted. A representation of violence can reiterate or challenge normalised social structures. I will explore this idea with the help of some examples in the sections that follow, in which I will argue that what is often missing from the debates about performed violence, whether they focus on spectators being endangered or offended, is an analysis of *ideology* and *performativity*.

Performative impacts

Performativity can be a confusing term, because the word *performative* is also sometimes used to mean 'in the manner of a performance'. Performativity, as a philosophical term and concept, is not the same as performance. It is a theory that explores how language and communication work, suggesting, for example, that words never merely *describe* the way things are. Instead we can argue that 'the way things are' is created and reinforced through language. Description is neither neutral nor separate from the things that it describes.

In her 1997 book *Excitable Speech: A Politics of the Performative*, Judith Butler explores this idea in the context of hate speech. She asks, 'What does it mean for a word not only to name, but also in some sense to perform and, in particular, to perform what it names?' (p. 43). Hate speech can be construed as an act of violence. If someone uses a racist or homophobic term of abuse, their use of that term draws on and takes power from a history of similar abuse (verbal, psychological and violently physical) against people of different races or sexualities. The abusive term is being used not to describe the person but to attack and oppress them. It isn't a description but an action, a violent action.

The fact that hate speech cites a history of oppression renders it powerful by connecting it with pre-existing structures and attitudes under which the victim of the abuse is already actually or potentially oppressed. The hateful language therefore constitutes oppression. It does not simply describe or refer to hatred and abuse; it embodies hatred and abuse, and its repetition creates and reiterates the circumstances that render some people powerful and others oppressed.

This idea can be applied to performance, and particularly to performances of simulated violence, in interesting ways. It is easy to think of performances as being representations of the world as it is or was or could be, or of the imaginary circumstances they depict. In this sense performance tends to be treated as descriptive rather than performative, certainly by many of the sociological studies that engage with the effects on spectators of watching performed violence.

But what can be gained by considering simulated violence from the perspective of what the representation (the act of showing) *does*?

Sarah Kane's play *Phaedra's Love* (Gate Theatre, London, 1996) concludes with a sequence of mob violence, during which a number of specific things happen. Kane's stage directions give precise instructions about what should be shown. The sequence is longer, and contains more dialogue and action, than the passage quoted below, but here is enough of it to make my point:

> Man 2 *holds* Hippolytus.
> Man 1 *takes a tie from around a child's neck and puts it around* Hippolytus' *throat.*
> *He strangles* Hippolytus, *who is kicked by the* Women *as he chokes into semi-consciousness.*
> Woman 2 *produces a knife.*
> Strophe: No! No! Don't hurt him, don't kill him!
> [...]
> Theseus *pulls* Strophe *away from* Woman 2 *who she is attacking.*
> *He rapes her.*
> *The crowd watch and cheer.*
> *When* Theseus *has finished he cuts her throat.*
> (p. 95)

There is a lot happening here, and much of it is precisely laid out by Kane. Initially it might seem that all the fight director has to do is follow her instructions. When a director is trying to stage the piece, however, a lot of questions become apparent that have not been answered in the stage directions.

How long should each action take? The sequence could race by in a few minutes, as it did in Kane's own production at the Gate Theatre in 1996. Or, as in Anne Tipton's 2005 production at the Bristol Old Vic, it could be extended to last around a quarter of an hour. The difference this makes to the way the audience experience the scene, and to the way the scene influences our reception of the play as a whole, is enormous. My experience watching the Bristol production was that everything that had come before, the seven scenes that lead up to and contextualise the explosion of violence at the end, was erased from my mind. On leaving the theatre I found it hard to remember anything other than the violence. The effect of this directorial choice was to make the play *about* the violence, a reductive and misleading reading of Kane's text.

Production decisions can affect audience experience, then. But what about their wider performative impact? For an example let us return to the idea of embodying norms and look in more detail at the choices involved in staging one line of Kane's stage directions – an instruction that comes up in many plays by different playwrights, in precisely these words: *He rapes her.*

Staging rape

The image of a rape is obviously an image of power and powerlessness (Kane emphasises this in *Phaedra's Love* by having the act take place before a cheering crowd). The image of a man raping a woman is an image of male power over a female body, and, furthermore, this power is linked directly to sex. Questions are immediately raised about the act of embodying such an image onstage. The spectators are not encountering 'rape' as an abstract concept; they are witnessing two actual bodies in that specific relationship of powerful sexual aggressor and powerless victim. The knowledge that the bodies belong to performers and that there is no actual rape taking place may make it possible to continue watching, but the embodiment of the idea 'rape' does make a difference to the way that it is understood.

Like an example of hate speech, a portrayal of rape might be said to refer to, draw on and draw strength from a history of men in positions of relative power attacking women through aggressive, non-consensual sex. Unlike hate speech, Kane's play was not constructed to reiterate and reinforce those oppressive power relationships, but an image of rape has such power that it can easily escape its context and come to dominate a spectator's experience of the performance. Fight directors, performers and directors have a responsibility to make their choices in such a way that the image of rape they create serves the narrative and political needs of the play but does not empower rapists or disempower their victims. They need to ensure that the image does not contribute to an understanding of the world in which the relationships between men and women in general can be reconciled with this idea of relative power and powerlessness.

How are the performers' bodies arranged in relation to one another? The Bristol production had Strophe on all fours with her back slightly arched, while Theseus knelt behind her with his body upright. To what extent are the performers' faces visible to the audience, and what are their expressions? In Bristol both faces were visible; his was predominantly angry, while she remained almost expressionless throughout. How much bodily movement is involved? Here Strophe was almost motionless. What happens to the performers' clothing? Theseus, in this production, remained fully covered but Strophe's trousers were torn off, so the woman's bare flesh was part of the image. The combined result of these decisions was an image of an angry and powerful man violently having sex from behind with an entirely passive, half-naked woman.

All these production decisions served to emphasise the dominance of the male rapist over his female victim, but there was also an unpleasant sense that the power dynamic being portrayed drew on referents other than rape. The choice to place Theseus behind Strophe while she put up no resistance implied possible complicity on her part, and the judgement offered by connecting complicity with rape is extremely problematic. In fact, all the choices made about the woman's part in this image drew on familiar, normalised assumptions to performatively reiterate the sexual oppression of women.

The rapist retained a degree of physical poise and composure throughout the act that went beyond an illustration of controlling aggressive power. He did not seem to be demeaned or diminished by the act; indeed, it initially increased his relative strength and status. In contrast, the woman's body was displayed to the audience in a position that cited common images from 'soft' pornography, a connection that was strengthened by her expressionless face and the decision to expose her naked legs and buttocks as the act was taking place.

These choices had a number of effects. The stage image cited a wider manifestation of power and oppression and harnessed it to the act of rape. The sexual oppression of women – the relentlessly sexualised portrayal of female bodies and the resultant reiteration of heterosexual male empowerment – was embodied in this image in the context of a violent rape. The wider effect of the image, beyond fulfilling Kane's stage direction, was not just to represent or describe a rape. It was to constitute rape as an act of male (hetero)sexual power that is able to sit relatively comfortably within existing social power relationships. Most importantly, it did so without subjecting this idea to scrutiny or challenge, and without drawing the audience's attention to what it was doing in any way.

While the example just cited is a particularly clear illustration of the performative issues surrounding simulations of rape, these are issues that don't just disappear with a different arrangement of bodies. Whether it is ever possible to embody a simulated rape without performatively citing a history of pornography and sexual oppression is a serious question that needs to be considered analytically and with full understanding of the performative implications of the decisions made.

Ideological implications

Clearly, without getting too distracted by the fascinating complexities of performativity, we can see that it offers a useful way of conceptualising the different levels at which a performed simulation of violence can work. In a similar way ideology is a useful conceptual framework within which to think about the performance of violence while avoiding the more problematic and circular aspects of causality.

Ideology is a way of thinking about power relationships and the habits and assumptions that work to keep power in the hands of the same individuals or groups at the expense of others. Terry Eagleton, in his 1976 book *Marxism and Literary Criticism*, describes ideologies as 'the ideas, values and feelings by which [people] experience their societies at various times', and he goes on to say that 'to understand ideologies is to understand both the past and the present more deeply; and such understanding contributes to our liberation' (p. viii). The perspective of ideology enables us to analyse the importance of power and its oppressive or liberatory implications – not just with respect to characters within a sequence of performed violence, but also in the context of the performance itself, in the relationships between the performance and its spectators, and in the wider critical responses that it generates.

The professional wrestling performances created by the US-based company World Wrestling Entertainment (WWE) provide a particularly interesting example of ideological performed violence. Professional (pro) wrestling is a hugely popular entertainment form. WWE shows are broadcast in well over fifty countries, and the company draws massive audiences to its live and televised events. The violent content of the shows has prompted ongoing protests that use causal arguments to express concern about pro wrestling being packaged as entertainment. Consideration of the shows' ideological function, however, opens up different avenues for analysis.

Pro wrestling is structured according to a clear set of regulatory principles. One is that whatever storyline-driven encounters are performed between characters, they always lead to fighting. Storylines are constructed to provide reasons for fighting to happen, but they do not have to offer justifications. No one would think of asking why these characters address their differences by fighting. Of course they do; this is wrestling. The structural centrality of the combat encounter reiterates the idea, familiar from global political contexts such as the post-9/11 'war on terror', that fighting is inevitable and necessary.

Another structural and ideological principle of pro wrestling is the division of characters into *faces* (a shortening of *babyfaces*), with whom the spectators identify, and *heels*, who are the objects of hatred, derision and sometimes disgust. This division is fundamental to the clear and successful functioning of the fights; almost every match pits a face wrestler against a heel. WWE makes precise use of stereotypes in its construction of characters, and this is important too. When stereotyped representations of particular social, national, ethnic, religious, class or political groups are positioned on either side of the face/heel divide, an ideological choice is being made.

WWE's performances perpetuate particular ways of viewing, understanding, empowering or disempowering certain individuals and groups within society. The ideological choices made by WWE consistently communicate the ideas that America is more powerful than the rest of the world, men are more powerful than women, male-dominated heterosexuality is the only acceptable form of sexual attraction, and certain body shapes are beautiful, while others (for example those with impairments) are freakish and ugly.

These ideological messages are strengthened by being enacted through violent encounters because there is both extremity and absolute clarity in this kind of violence. The victors and the vanquished are clearly identifiable at the end of each encounter. The ideological codes of wrestling (where there is honour in strength, stamina and the ability to absorb pain, but dishonour in cowardice and weakness) are rendered legible through each moment of the fight. Spectators learn from the performances and from one another's responses that particular behaviours or identities deserve to be violently suppressed. Of course, these ideological perspectives are not unique to WWE. In fact, what is important here is that WWE harnesses specific power structures that are pre-existent and recognisable; it wouldn't work if it didn't. Spectators are already familiar with the social scripts that they cite, and so the embodiment and violent enactment of recognisable power relationships in such extreme ways serves to reinforce oppressive social and political norms.

These observations demonstrate the ways in which an ideological perspective can help us analyse the implications of a particular form of performed violence without getting caught up in the sometimes hysterical responses generated by causal arguments. We are not simply asking, 'Does watching this material make us more likely to be violent ourselves or to accept violence in others?' Instead we can use our analysis to explore what this specific manifestation of entertainment violence teaches us about the world. We can use it to identify existing power structures and we can ask, 'Does this material reinforce, obscure or offer a challenge to the way that power is distributed and used in contexts beyond the performance?' An ideological analysis can help us examine what contributes to a sense that violence is the norm, something inevitable, 'human nature' or 'the way things are'.

Pro wrestling is a good example of performed violence that is controversial – it provokes ferocious disapproval and equally fierce support. If we consider how ubiquitous the representation of violence is in theatre and performance, however, it is striking that most of it does not generate controversy or protest. While the first performances of *Saved*, *The Romans in Britain* and *Blasted* were both denounced and celebrated for their simulated acts of violence, the majority of plays contain plenty of violence that goes unmentioned. If the former examples get discussed in terms of what is and is not acceptable, we should now ask why most performed violence is usually not questioned in this way.

History and canonical violence

Particular plays are frequently cited as being 'classic' or 'important'. Often the same dramatic texts are presented as exemplary of a particular period or genre and are taught in curricula across most schools and universities. Shakespeare's *Hamlet* comes immediately to mind. Other familiar texts might be Sophocles' *Oedipus Rex*, Henrik Ibsen's *A Doll's House,* Arthur Miller's *Death of a Salesman* and Samuel Beckett's *Endgame*. These plays, along with certain others, form a *canon*, an authoritative collection of works that are widely understood to be the 'most significant' plays across the span of (in this example) Western European and North American theatre history.

Because they are treated as both important and exemplary, canonical texts tend to be performed and studied more frequently than other dramatic works. While their content and historical context are subjected to ongoing analysis, their canonical status, once established, is less commonly questioned. Although many canonical texts were radical and controversial in their original contexts, their presence in the canon indicates wide critical acceptance and a status that could be described as both mainstream and highbrow. In this context, any depictions of violence these plays contain tend to be similarly rendered acceptable.

Much of the ideological status of the canon comes from its relation to history, and history is itself most usually written and communicated in canonical form. Historians speak of *grand narratives*, or overarching representations of events that tell the story of a particular period in broad, general terms. The representation of English history as a monarchical progression, divided up into the reigns of different kings and queens, is a good example of this. So is the identification of particular periods and/or places with selected key events. It is worth noting that these designated events are often wars, revolutions, assassinations or other acts of violence.

At this point I am going to suggest that certain types of violence, and certain ways of presenting and contextualising violence in performance, have a canonical status that tends to evade serious analytical questioning. Clearly the whole concept of a selective canon, granting acceptance and significance to specific texts, suggests again the existence of particular structures of power. There is an ideology at work here that needs to be identified and analysed.

The idea that history can be measured out according to acts of violence is the first point to consider. In terms of a historical grand narrative, circumstances often change very clearly as a result of violent events. The execution of Charles I in England, the revolutions in France and Russia, the first and second world wars, the atomic bombing of Hiroshima and Nagasaki, the attacks on the World Trade Center in New York – these events are easily identified with social and political change, and so they often come to be used as shorthand for referring to those changes. Violence has an enormous impact on the people and societies who experience it, and this, too, lends historical significance to wars, revolutions, genocides and so on. Much of the canon of history is composed of violent events, and it would be safe to say that few would find this surprising.

When we come to consider violence and performance, we can also see that violence re-told and imagined (as distinct from being actually experienced) is dramatic and exciting. Just as it does in the theatre, violence in the narratives of history provides not only structure but also an imaginative hook that keeps us involved. Whether it is imagining suffering, motivation or technique/method, the process of thinking about violence from a distance can be especially engaging.

Staging history through re-enactment

An interesting point of connection between the telling of history and the act of performing is the practice of historical re-enactment. Many museums employ actors whose job is to enliven the exhibitions through performance interpretation. The Royal Armouries museum in Leeds, UK, has a whole department of specialist interpreters who use their knowledge of fighting to explore and explain how individual weapons would have been used and how people probably fought in different times, places and contexts. But on a much larger scale than these professional performance interpretations are the multitude of societies whose members involve themselves in immersive participatory re-enactments of aspects of a particular historical period.

The Sealed Knot is a UK-based society focused on using re-enactment to research and educate a wide public about life during the English Civil War. Its members are interested in all aspects of seventeenth-century daily life and offer demonstrations of cooking, crafts, clothing and so on during the course of an afternoon or a weekend gathering, but the centrepiece of most events is a re-enactment of a battle. Participants, on foot or on horseback, perform fighting with muskets, pikes and cannons according to a careful plan but with scope for plenty of less-planned individual encounters on the field of battle. Spectators experience great sensory excitement as the noise, smoke and visual chaos of the battle unfolds before their eyes. What they are witnessing is a spectacular live performance that represents a canonical moment of historical violence.

In ideological terms there is much to ponder here. Primarily, of course, participatory re-enactment is about enjoyment as well as experiential education. Re-enactments of violence are therefore always likely to sanitise or diminish the suffering, horror, dirt and squalor that are inseparable from any actual battlefield. These aspects of violence are not exciting or enjoyable to imagine. The enjoyment, for participants and spectators, comes from engaging with fighting as play. This is not to suggest that members of the Sealed Knot are not serious or thorough in their research or its application. However, while no one would expect or want combat re-enactors actually to experience the danger and trauma of battle, its removal from the experience is significant because it permits participants and spectators untroubled enjoyment of the violence. Much of the need or desire to imagine consequences is removed by the nature of the performance.

Like pro wrestling, combat re-enactment is self-justifying. It provides its own context. These battles, these acts of violence, are being performed because history tells us they happened. They are being re-enacted, re-shown, re-imagined here and now because that is what historical re-enactors do. They are deemed educational and important because they are representations of history.

This logic has the potential to circumvent analysis. The argument runs thus: this is what we know happened – therefore this is what we show – therefore this is what we know happened. There is little scope here for alternative readings or contextual critical perspectives. 'History' has a status that, when connected with performance in this way, precludes challenge and judgement. The contemplation of implications and alternatives can find little space in the spectacular excitement and participatory enjoyment of a battle re-enactment. The term *re-enactment* is the important indicator here. This is not about questioning but about striving for authenticity, and because of this it has the potential to deny other questions. In this context violence, because it is historical fact, comes to seem inevitable.

Canonical plays can do a similar thing, presenting particular behaviours, attitudes and relationships as inevitable by implication, or as exempt from questioning because of the canonical and historical status of the text. The plays of Shakespeare (perhaps the ultimate canonical playwright) have been critiqued on this basis from various perspectives. Feminist and post-colonial readings, for example, have explored the ways in which power relationships between men and women, and between European and non-European individuals and countries, are constituted in the plays. The difference here between productions of plays and historical re-enactment performances is that theatre offers far more scope for different perspectives, analyses and judgements to be explored through a range of production choices. Historical authenticity is not usually the most important factor in a production of a Shakespeare play, and many productions have looked for opportunities to highlight and examine the ideological questions and problems contained within these dramatic texts.

What is important about this is that ideological patterns have to be recognised before they can be examined. Postcolonial and feminist perspectives have drawn attention to particular patterns, and while no one would suggest that the result has been a complete shift in attitude and behaviour, the awareness has at least enabled an ongoing process of critique. Representations of violence are undeniably connected with power relationships, and it is interesting to consider which of the ideological structures on which they are built are generally recognised and analysed. An example from Shakespeare might help us unpack this idea.

The ideological code of honour

Romeo and Juliet, like many other plays, poems and stories, is embedded within the history of duelling, which was born out of the related conceptual tradition of honour. Duelling has deep historical roots. Personal duels, in which two individuals fought one another with agreed weapons according to agreed rules, were common during the heyday of Western European chivalry (roughly spanning the period between the eleventh and fifteenth centuries) and continued through to the eighteenth century and, with less frequency, beyond. Duels were a way of achieving and maintaining status within the social structures of predominantly masculine nobility. Particular kinds of insult or injury were considered a threat to the honour of a nobleman that could be remedied only through a duel. Honour and combat were, for men, inextricable throughout much of European history.

Honour was, and still is, a fascinating and rather slippery concept. In another of Shakespeare's plays, *Henry IV Part 1*, Sir John Falstaff discusses the personal dangers involved in preserving one's honour by fighting and the lack of practical use honour has to a man who has died to preserve it:

> Can honour set-to a leg? No. Or an arm? No.
> Or take away the grief of a wound? No. Honour
> hath no skill in surgery, then? No. What is honour? A word. What is in that word 'honour'? Air.
> A trim reckoning! Who hath it? He that died o'
> Wednesday. Doth he feel it? No. Doth he hear
> it? No. 'Tis insensible then? Yea, to the dead.
> But will it not live with the living? No. Why?
> Detraction will not suffer it. Therefore I'll none
> of it. Honour is a mere scutcheon. And so ends
> my catechism. (5.1.130–40)

But Falstaff is a coward, and his reasoned argument against honour would have found little sympathy among the aristocratic men of his – or Shakespeare's – time. That honour was gained through courageous fighting, lost through failure to avenge insults and preserved or regained in single combat was absolutely part of the conceptual framework that shaped the Western European tradition. And this concept is still current in many contexts, in fact – for example as the ideological structure that supports WWE storylines and performances.

Romeo and Juliet addresses the concept in an interesting way. The ancient feud of honour between the two families is presented as a bad thing, and the deaths of young men through duelling is certainly subjected to criticism. However, there is no possibility within the play's story for its characters not to fight. In fact it is Romeo's refusal to fight Tybalt that causes Mercutio's death, since Mercutio feels he must step in to counteract Romeo's 'calm, dishonourable, vile submission' (3.1.66). Mercutio, as he dies, blames the feud for his fatal injury: 'A plague a'both your houses! They have made worms' meat of me' (3.1.97–98). He does not blame himself for fighting, or offer any challenge to the honour codes of duelling that made the fight, for him, unavoidable.

This aspect of the play is often not explored in twenty-first-century productions. The play's tragedy is that Romeo and Juliet are innocent victims of the violent feud between their families. It is possible to offer a pacifist reading of the play in this context, and it is particularly important in such a reading to recognise the moment when Capulet and Montague finally learn from the lovers' deaths that violence and revenge lead only to sorrow. However, the insidious details of the ideological code of honour are rarely analysed more directly when *Romeo and Juliet* is performed.

The concept of honour and the practice of duelling are so familiar and accepted as to be canonical in themselves. They are also mechanisms through which particular behaviours, values and power structures are maintained – and, again, these are not always directly connected to violence. In her book *Manhood and the Duel* (2003) Jennifer A. Low argues that the regulated concepts and practices associated with fighting for honour functioned culturally to perpetuate fixed, recognisable power relationships between men and women, and between different social ranks, which became increasingly significant as these relationships grew less stable in society.

There is an important point here. Theatrical representations of violence can often be ideologically reactionary, functioning to reaffirm power structures that may be being threatened, questioned or challenged. As we have seen, this reaffirmation often occurs at a deeper level than the narrative context given to the violence, and reactionary portrayals can therefore make social change harder to achieve. When we analyse performed representations of violence, or make choices about how to stage violence in our own performances, it is important to consider the ways in which the portrayal connects with existing ideological questions. It is also important to recognise instances of canonical or historical status potentially obscuring the importance of what that act of showing does.

Actuality and simulation

It should be clear by now that fundamental to many of the debates about theatre and violence is the relationship between performance and actuality. Causal arguments require this distinction to be clear in order to assess the degree and direction of influence between performed/virtual violence in entertainment contexts and criminal/political violence in social, national and international contexts. Performative and ideological perspectives complicate the connection by considering ways in which a representation, although not in itself an act of violence, might respond to or constitute an ideology that has actually violent effects. Violence and performance are inextricably linked in a relationship that cannot be reduced to clear concepts of 'real' and 'pretend'.

To analyse different forms of performed and simulated violence, it is important to move beyond simple causality in our consideration of what is enacted, how it is enacted, by whom and in what contexts. As an example, let us explore an analytical contrast between the performed and the virtual in two generic examples of simulated violent action.

Stage combat and gaming

The practice of stage combat requires performers and fight directors to develop a degree of understanding about actual violence, its techniques and its effects. Good fight directors know about anatomy, not just so that they can match up simulated cause with performed effect, but also because they must ensure that the performers' bodies remain safe and protected from actual harm. They also know about fighting. An Equity-registered fight director in the UK is required to have qualified to high standards in at least one martial art and as a fencer; many have also studied other forms of actual fighting from different places, traditions and historical periods. It is obvious but worth stating: in order to stage violence it is necessary to know about it.

Imagine this sequence in performance. At the climax of a heated argument, character A (the aggressor) pushes character V (the victim) so hard and unexpectedly that he falls to the floor. Before he is able to get up, she is standing over him and has grabbed him by the hair. As he screams and tries to loosen her grip she shakes him roughly from side to side and throws him back to the ground. She grabs him by the throat and begins to throttle him; he chokes and kicks, struggles against her and eventually manages to break her hold, throwing her off so he can roll away out of reach. They stare at each other across the stage, both gasping for breath, their two bodies racing with adrenaline.

What is it like to watch this sequence as a member of the audience? The explosion of violence is sudden; although it has been set up by an escalating verbal argument it still takes me by surprise. It is fast, a change in pace that shifts my perspective and alters the nature of my engagement. As the violent action moves across the stage, I turn my head to follow it. Maybe I shift forward in my seat. Perhaps my heart beats a little faster, and as the victim struggles for breath I might feel my own airways constrict slightly in an imaginative echo of his experience. Or maybe, responding to the aggressor, I feel in my own hands the imagined sensation of squeezing a throat: an unsettling moment of identification. As the victim escapes the suffocating grip of his antagonist I feel relief, a relief that is emphasised and extended as, in the breathless pause that follows, I become aware of the surge of adrenaline my own body has just experienced in this moment of engagement between spectator and performance.

I have been utterly absorbed in the violent action, yet at no point in all this have I thought that actor V was actually being throttled. If we put aside for the moment those performances that deliberately blur the distinction between simulated and actual violence, it is fair to say that in the majority of plays and films the spectators know without question that the violence portrayed is not actually inflicted on or by the performers who portray it. With this knowledge comes the assumption and acceptance of trickery. If the violence seemed convincing but I know it did not really cause pain or do harm, then the performers must have done something in that moment to deceive my perceptions. As a spectator I know this, but that knowledge does not usually prevent me from experiencing the physical and emotional impact of the performance.

So what are the actors doing to create these illusions and provoke such responses in their spectators? Stage combat is a collaborative practice. Actors work together to create illusions of aggression, antagonism and the loss of physical control. Two of the principles that underpin much stage violence are the reversal of energy and victim control. Let's consider one example of each from the imaginary stage fight described above.

The principle of victim control is that the performer whose character is on the receiving end of the violent act is actually in control of the collaborative movement. When character A shakes character V by the hair, actor A is not initiating any of the movements. The appearance of being shaken is entirely created by the actor playing the victim, while actor A, the illusory aggressor, simply follows his movements.

Of course, the skill involved in this reversal of control is considerable. The aggressor must seem to be the forceful cause of the victim's uncontrolled movements, and so actor A has to produce the appearance of pulling without doing so, visibly engaging her muscles but not using them to pull. Actor V must not only remain in control of his own movements while appearing not to be, but also do this in a way that enables actor A to move with him. If he takes her by surprise, if she cannot stay with him, the illusion will be spoilt.

The second principle, reversal of energy, works in a similar way. In an actual act of strangulation, the aggressor would place her hands around the victim's neck and squeeze to tighten her grip. She would use her body weight to push inwards and downwards on the throat of her victim in order to restrict or shut off his supply of air. In performance, the actor's throat must be protected from squeezing or pushing, yet the illusion of strength and struggle needs force and energy to power the movements.

The solution once again is for the actors to do the opposite of the action they are portraying. They reverse the direction of the energy. Once actor A's hands are safely in position, actor V can grab them with his own hands, giving the impression that he is trying to break her grip. Then, instead of the aggressor sending her energy inwards towards the victim's throat, she pulls outwards. It is the actor portraying the victim who pulls the aggressor's hands towards him. Genuine muscular effort is applied to the action. The illusion is convincing and compelling for spectators because it is created through actual physical energy.

The principles and techniques of stage combat offer a useful perspective from which to analyse actuality and simulation in performed violence. Recognising some of the processes by which illusory violence can be simulated by performers and received by spectators enables us to delve more precisely into issues of intention and reception, cause and effect, acting technique, spectatorial engagement and the impact, implications and possible functions of violence in theatre and performance.

Computer game violence is a form of simulation in which the roles of performer and spectator are to some extent merged. The experience of watching performed violence is contextualised through the simultaneous experience of controlling and enacting the simulation. There is a seeming collision here between simulation and actuality as well as between performer and spectator, as the gamer's actual actions create the simulation/performance of the game. The character or avatar is a simulation of a person, not a real person. Yet it is a manifestation of the actual gamer in the world of the game; it acts as the gamer, under the gamer's control, with no agency of its own.

In a first-person interactive computer game, the gamer enacts violence (through an avatar–character) on a simulated victim or foe with the intention to cause harm. The gamer and the character have the same intention in this scenario, and it is a violent one. In the playful context of the computer game, however, the violent action takes place as simulation, because the victim is another character or avatar. First-person computer game violence could be said to allow the gamer to play with and enact violent intentions safely, in the assurance that they cannot result in actual harm. The safety – the guarantee of non-harm – comes from the fact that the victim is not real.

In stage combat, the characters' intentions are violent but the actors' are not; the performers and their actions are themselves the guarantee of non-harm. We have seen how stage combat requires the character's violent intention to be replaced in the actor by an intention to protect the safety of the other party. Spectators, whether or not they understand how it is done, generally know this and rely on it. The context of a play in a theatre also guarantees non-harm and so enables the violent actions and intentions to be playfully, imaginatively and seriously explored.

Actual violence as performance

Of course, stage combat is not the only form in which violence is presented in theatre. Within theatre and performance, the clarity of the distinction between simulated and actual violence, and the nature of violent harm, is also frequently challenged. The simulated aggressive fighting in professional wrestling is created through acts of collaborative and non-aggressive, but still actual, violence. Actual violence is sometimes structured and enacted as performance, as with ultimate fighting and mixed martial arts shows or historical gladiatorial combat. Some performance artists, sometimes known as body artists, inflict actual violent harm on their bodies as an act of performance.

In Mike Parr's 2002 performance *Close the Concentration Camps* (Monash University Museum of Art, Melbourne) the artist/performer's body was branded and his lips were sewn shut. As the title of the work suggests, there was a direct political intention behind this display of actual violence by and against the performer. Parr was responding to the reported suffering of asylum seekers who, held for extended periods in isolated Australian detention centres, were using acts of self-harm to draw attention to and protest against their treatment. In an article discussing this performance, Rand Hazou includes a quote from Parr on the political function of his body art: 'you can't represent the plight of people in detention centres by doing a painting or a drawing. It's trivial by comparison with the extreme reality' ('Dys-appearance and Compassion', 2010, p. 155).

This notion of the failure of simulation is an interesting one. Parr's observation suggests that to respond to actual suffering with simulated representation is to trivialise reality. This argument might well seem to sound the death knell for performance, but there is a serious concern here about the politics and ethics of simulation, which it is worth considering from both sides.

Parr's performance, and the performances of other violent body artists, work in part by utilising the shock of the real. In a context in which simulation and representation are usually assumed and unquestioned, the intervention of actuality has a jarring effect, shifting the perspective and provoking different ways of thinking about and responding to the event. In this respect it certainly could be argued that Parr's 'expression of solidarity and empathy' (p. 155) with the suffering of the asylum seekers would have been less powerful if the violence against his body had been simulated. Part of the point of this work was to bring the suffering into the world of the gallery-goers, to require a direct witnessing of physical violence and bodily harm that otherwise remained hidden in the far-off detention centres.

However, it is also clear that this 'expression of solidarity and empathy' does not replicate the suffering of the asylum seekers, and the spectators know this. Parr has freedom and agency. He chooses to inflict this violence on himself, and to invite others to watch. In doing so, he is attempting to implicate spectators in the asylum seekers' suffering as well as to provoke their horrified empathy.

As the spectators watch the violence against the artist's body in the gallery, they are encouraged to consider the ways in which public passivity enables and implicitly supports acts of political violence in the world beyond. But watching a performance is not the same as being witness to violence in other contexts. A performance or an artwork is conventionally allowed to progress uninterrupted by its spectators, who assume that the creators of the work are in control of its progress, and that the participants have knowingly consented to the actions in which they are involved. The ethics of spectatorship are conventionally different from those of witnessing in non-performance contexts.

One body artist who has famously explored this territory is Marina Abramović, whose 1974 performance *Rhythm 0* (Studio Morra, Naples) saw her hand over control completely to her spectators. She set up a table covered with objects ranging from a feather, a rose and some honey to a scalpel, a gun and a bullet. She then remained impassive in the space for six hours, during which the spectators were free to do what they wished with her and with the objects.

In a short interview available on the Museum of Modern Art (MoMA) web site, Abramović remembers how people initially interacted gently with her but then, as the show progressed and she made no response to anything they did, became increasingly nastier and more violent in their interventions. She describes having her clothes and then her body cut with the scalpel, a spectator cutting her neck and drinking her blood, and how eventually someone put the bullet in the pistol, placed it in Abramović's hand, put it against her head and began to squeeze the trigger, 'to see if I would resist'. At the conclusion of the six hours, she recalls, when the end of the show was announced, 'everybody ran away – literally ran out of the door'.

Clearly this was a performance that was designed to provoke extreme responses in its audience, and to explore the nature and limits of consent and the boundaries of performance. By placing herself in the space under those circumstances the artist was giving permission for interaction; however, her passivity seemed to render it up to the spectator–participants themselves to decide how far it was acceptable or possible to go. The show was an ethical challenge to its spectators, although not necessarily a fair one, as it was also a performance designed to encourage the exploration and testing of boundaries. The spectator who put the gun to the artist's head may well have assumed that eventually she *would* resist, that the rules not just of performance but of human, social or even legal interaction dictated that Abramović would not actually allow herself to be murdered by a member of her audience.

Beyond performance

The ideas explored so far suggest that rather than offering a clear 'either/or' duality, the relationship between simulation and actuality in performance might form more of a continuum. A performed act of violence may be entirely simulated: planned, structured, choreographed and rehearsed to create the illusion of harm while preserving the safety of the actors, as with stage combat. In other contexts, such as pro wrestling, the violence may be simulated but the techniques used have much greater impact on the bodies of the performers, with pain and bodily harm incorporated into the process as part of the way the simulation is made. Body art takes actual acts of bodily violence and frames them to be contemplated aesthetically, and often also politically, as art; the defining point here seems to be not so much a question of simulation versus actuality but of knowledge, control and consent. Finally, of course, many sports present competitive fights to audiences, sometimes surrounding the bouts of fighting with elements of ritual (as with sumo wrestling, for example) or more theatrical, showy elements, such as can be seen at major boxing matches.

When we consider simulation and actuality in this way we are measuring what is real according to the nature of the harm done to, or risked by, the bodies of the performers. Alongside this comes consideration of the intention of the performers (to harm or to protect, for example), and the extent to which they have consented to and are in control of the bodily violence they experience. Finally, when we introduce competitive martial sport into the discussion, we also come across the question of pre-determination. We would expect the actors (and perhaps much of the audience) to know in advance the outcome of the final duel in *Hamlet*, but the pre-determined results of pro wrestling generate much of the playful relationship between this performance form and its spectators. When watching a boxing match, on the other hand, we assume that the outcome is being decided, moment by moment, in an unplanned fight. This might lead us to class boxing as 'actual' in contrast to the simulations of stage combat and pro wrestling.

I have also considered the idea that simulated violence, framed and consumed as performance, might have actual implications and effects. Again there was a sense of continuum rather than simple duality here, particularly as the discussion moved away from direct violence-to-violence causality and explored wider ideological effects connected with power relationships and situations of political, social or cultural inequality.

The majority of the ideas and perspectives considered so far have begun with performance and looked outwards from there, although I have attempted to render this linearity more complex as the discussion has progressed. I have tried, for example, to complicate the familiar causal suspicion that performances of violence lead to further violence in society at large by suggesting that performed acts of violence often reflect, explore and offer the space to contemplate an already violent world. The final sections of this book will continue to explore the continuums of causality and actuality, but with the focus now on actual violence taking place beyond acknowledged venues and contexts of performance. Beginning with actual events, we will explore a few ways in which performance has been used to help people understand and respond to the horrific effects and implications of acts of real violence.

Spectacle and terrorism

The first approach I will consider is theoretically driven and involves a familiar strategy from the discipline of Performance Studies, whereby the idea of performance is used as a tool for analysing actual events and actions. Perhaps the clearest example of this from recent history – certainly the most extensively discussed in English-language scholarship – is the example with which I began this book: the attack on the World Trade Center in New York on 11 September 2001.

The hijacking of passenger aircraft which were then flown into Manhattan's iconic 'Twin Towers' was an act of violence on a large scale. It resulted in actual deaths and actual destruction. It also created the fear of further attacks, perhaps a sense of vulnerability not experienced before, among many of the people who witnessed the attacks either in person or more widely through the television, internet and print media. It was quickly named an act of *terrorism*, which can be understood to indicate an act of violence deliberately designed to achieve a wider effect than its immediate toll in terms of lives lost and bodies injured. Terrorism in this context is identified as much with the dissemination of the image of the violent event as it is with the actual violence. The image extends and repeats outwards, reaching a wide audience and reiterating the fear generated by the original act.

This act of 'terrorist' violence was also an act of spectacle, of imagery – we might say, of choreographed violent action. It caught the public imagination not just because of its individual victims but because of its large scale, the iconic nature of the buildings it destroyed and its wide range of symbolic possibilities. It also left behind its site of destruction as a second spectacle to be visited and viewed, and it is important to remember how much significance has been accorded to decisions about the medium- and long-term future of the 'Ground Zero' site.

Yet to return to Adriana Cavarero's analysis, there is an aspect of horror here, too, and it is possible that the endless repetition of the images of the attacks via news and other media contributed to this aspect of their reception. How many times can the flight instinct – the terror response – be engaged before it is replaced by the paralysis of horror? There might be avenues of exploration here for politicians and theatre scholars alike. The difference between active and passive reception is a perennial point of focus for playwrights, theatre-makers, spectators and critics.

It is important to be clear that to discuss the 9/11 attacks or any act of spectacular actual violence in terms of performance is not to suggest that they are in any way less 'real'. Scholars who frame spectacular violence in this way are not subscribing to conspiracy theories or attempting to reduce the seriousness of the violence. When we analyse performance we think about images and how they are constructed, and we consider both specific intended effects and widely spiralling implications. We can focus on the particular strategies that the performance employs in order to achieve its various effects, and we can also consider the responses that it generates both in its immediate aftermath and later. It is both possible and useful to apply these analytical approaches to certain acts and events of violence, not in order to claim that they are *the same* as performances in theatres, but rather to recognise and come to understand some of the complex ways in which they function and the wide effects they can have.

We have seen that the analysis of violence is an analysis of power. Physical violence is a process through which power and powerlessness are inscribed on and through bodies. The previous example shows how large-scale destruction and multiple victims can have a series of spectacular effects, asserting the destructive power of the initially anonymous and even intangible aggressor not just over the specific victims of the particular act but much more widely over all who watch. Part of the spectatorial experience here is the realisation of vulnerability: that one of the suffering bodies could have been mine, and might be mine in the feared next attack. The intention here is to position the attacker(s) as powerful and the spectators (not just the immediate victims) as powerless.

Large-scale spectacle is about size and numbers and the suddenness of the event rather than individual examples of specific suffering; the focus on individuals that followed the 9/11 attacks was initiated by the media and the government after the event, and not by the attackers or the event itself. As a contrast let us consider an example of the violence/power paradigm that is focused individually, specifically and, crucially, slowly.

The suffering body as spectacle

The hunger strike is a historically familiar form of protest that is often associated with powerlessness. Hunger strikers are the victims of a violence that is literally imposed by themselves on their own bodies. However, in many cases the message of the hunger strike is that another violence, invisible because it is hidden or ignored, is being imposed on the victim from outside. The victim's attack on his own body can often be read as a process of rendering that hidden violence visible.

Hunger strikers display their own suffering bodies as spectacle. Since it generally takes a long time for a person to starve to death, the spectacle of harm is the slowly ongoing degeneration of the protestor's body. Here there is no sudden surprise, no explosion of violent action. In contrast to other forms of violence, deliberate starvation can appear to be a violence of inaction, although witnesses are unlikely to escape the awareness of the strength required to maintain inactivity in this context.

Hunger strikes are durational spectacles, then, in which the witness is required to notice detail, to identify gradual as well as more sudden changes in the appearance of the victim over time. Witnesses judge suffering by its appearance on the body of the victim. As the effects of slow starvation become more physically apparent, many witnesses may be provoked to imagine the sensations associated with such physical suffering. This act of imagination, when it happens, is an act of engagement in which the victim is perceived as an individual and as a fellow human.

However, the spectatorial processes involved in seeing and responding to other people's suffering are not as straightforward as pure physical empathy. In her book *The Body in Pain: The Making and Unmaking of the World* (1985), theorist Elaine Scarry argues that pain is not only invisible but also virtually impossible to describe to, or to be imagined and understood by, a person other than the one who is experiencing it. We can try to recognise another's pain and suffering by responding to its visible effects as they are manifested on the sufferer's body, but pain is by no means always visible in this way. The hunger striker (or any person starving, for whatever reason) is likely to be experiencing excruciating pain long before the visible effects of emaciation communicate 'suffering' to those watching.

Pain, as Scarry explains, is resistant to language. We cannot describe pain without resorting to what she calls a 'language of agency'. In other words, the experience of pain can be verbalised only in words that refer to weapons or attacks. We use words such as *burning*, *pounding* or *splitting* to describe our pain: adjectives that communicate violent actions which are not actually the cause of the pain we are attempting to verbalise. We might say something like 'It feels as if my head is being hit with a hammer' or 'I feel as if I'm being stabbed in the stomach': descriptions of imaginary weapons that, again, are not in actuality associated with the pain we feel. There are no words for pain that has no visible or tangible source, and because of this, pain and bodily suffering are difficult to communicate, imagine and empathetically share. Once the effects of suffering are embodied, as with the emaciated body of the hunger striker, the imaginative connection is somewhat easier to begin and to maintain.

Embodiment and witnessing

A hunger strike is an example of actual violence, but theatre and performance are also engaged with embodiment and visibility and can be used to strong political effect. For nine days in 2003 in Manchester, UK, artist Jai Redman built an installation artwork that could equally well be described as a durational performance. His expressed intention was to use aspects of liveness, physical presence and actuality as a way of countering the apathy and stasis that he felt were characteristic of public responses in the UK to the 'war on terror'. In particular Redman was concerned about Camp X-Ray, one of the US military internment camps at the Guantanamo Bay base in Cuba, where suspected terrorists were held for years without being formally tried.

Images from Camp X-Ray were iconic yet commonplace in the news media: chained prisoners in orange jumpsuits, their heads covered with bags, kneeling on the ground beside wire cages; barbed-wire fences adorned with the US flag and presidential seal; soldiers with guns stationed in observation towers. Redman felt that the ubiquity and familiarity of these media images were causing people to stop thinking about the actual experiences of detainees in the camp, many of whom had not been proved to be involved in terrorist activities. He therefore built a replica of the camp in a field in Greater Manchester and populated it with volunteer performers who took the roles of guards and prisoners.

Redman had no personal experience of detention at Guantanamo Bay, so every detail of his replica was drawn from media images and the descriptions that were widely available on the internet. In this sense, he had access only to the same information as his audience. The volunteer 'prisoners' ate the kinds of food provided for detainees in the actual camp, were often hooded and had the same restrictions on space and liberty. Spectators were free to watch through the fence, and to interact to a certain extent with the performers. The installation was not ticketed but rather was placed in a public space for people to notice, engage with and respond to at will.

Redman was concerned that for most people a general familiarity with images of the camp had replaced any real sense of the violence of incarceration that they portrayed. His *This Is Camp X-Ray* installation gave form to that violence through performers and physical space, allowing spectators to contemplate its actual physical existence. The performance was a response both to actual violence in a distant country and to the distancing and stasis-inducing effects of the repetition of the televised image. It was intended to be political and provocative, to initiate conversation and to make people aware of their own capacity to consume an image without contemplating its actual, embodied source.

In her book *Regarding the Pain of Others* (2003), Susan Sontag considers the role of the spectator who looks at (or turns away from) images of violence, suffering and pain. 'Harrowing photographs do not inevitably lose their power to shock,' she argues:

> But they are not much use if the task is to understand. Narratives can make us understand. Photographs do something else: they haunt us. Consider one of the unforgettable images of the war in Bosnia, a photograph of which the *New*

York Times foreign correspondent John Kifner wrote: 'The image is stark, one of the most enduring of the Balkan wars: a Serb militiaman casually kicking a dying Muslim woman in the head. It tells you everything you need to know.' But of course it doesn't tell us everything we need to know. (p. 80)

Of course, *This Is Camp X-Ray* didn't tell us everything we need to know about Guantanamo Bay, let alone about the 'war on terror' as a whole. Interestingly, it also resisted the construction of a narrative beyond what was available already from news reports and through the interpretation of images. What it did offer its audience was the opportunity to recognise and contemplate the knowledge that these familiar images from a distant place depicted real people having an ongoing experience. Iconic images or image sequences may 'haunt us', but in doing so they are divorced from time and thereby from experience. By recreating Camp X-Ray in actual space and time, Jai Redman and his colleagues relocated the images as experience and refocused spectatorial attention on the variously violent narratives that underpinned and contextualised those images.

Another example of a performance structured around the embodiment and witnessing of actual suffering is Yael Farber and Duma Kumalo's play *He Left Quietly* (National Festival of Arts, Grahamstown, South Africa, 2002), one of three 'testimonial plays' published together under the title *Theatre as Witness*. In these plays, black South African actors performed as themselves in dramas written and directed by Farber but based on their own stories of living under the Apartheid regime. As the play opens Kumalo, as actor and character, addresses the audience directly:

> When does the soul leave the body? .... At which precise moment?
> Does it leave with our last breath? .... Or the final beat of our heart? [...]
> In my life I have died many times. But here I am again and again – alive.
> I am Duma Joshua Kumalo. Prisoner number V 34-58. In 1984 I was condemned to death for a crime I did not commit.
> I spent three years on Death Row, and a further four years of a Life Sentence. I have been measured for the length of my coffin; the size of the rope for my neck; I took my last sacrament; I said – to my broken father – a final goodbye. (*Smiling gently.*) And with each of these moments, my soul left my body behind. The dead leave the living with a burden. When going to their deaths – they would shout to us: Those who survive – tell the world! (pp. 188–89)

Under Apartheid, acts of violence and oppression were insti-tutionalised in the laws and power structures of the coun-try, and many thousands of people suffered and participated in these acts. With the end of the regime came celebration but also the recognition that here was a country traumatised by its history. In an interview included in the same volume, Farber discusses her work in these terms:

> Put very simply, I profoundly believe that speaking is a form of healing. Until you've told your story – even if you intellectually understand you've been wronged – the memories may remain a source of secrecy, pain or shame. Speaking and being heard is a modest but profound beginning. The shattered history of South Africa will take generations to heal, but I believe theatre has a significant role in this process. (p. 24)

For Farber, the lived experience of actual violence needs to be told. Kumalo's cry 'Those who survive – tell the world!' encapsulates this sense that it is through the acts of telling and of listening to stories of violence that healing can begin and the hope of preventing future violence can arise. It is crucial to note the importance attached to the audience in this process. It is not just that victims need to tell, in a therapeutic context, about their experiences. Equally for Farber the spectators need to hear, to see, to experience the story themselves in order that the wider social trauma of violence can begin to be addressed.

Conclusion

In their 2009 book *Performance in Place of War*, James Thompson, Jenny Hughes and Michael Balfour discuss a wide range of theatre and performance practice taking place in circumstances directly contextualised by war. This does not exclude performances that take place at a distance from the actual violence: *This Is Camp X-Ray* is one of the many projects discussed in the book. However, the issue of closeness to/distance from the immediate place and time of violence is fundamental to the analysis offered by these authors. The book is structured in a way that:

> takes 'space/place' and 'time' as its organising principle. It explores how shifts in place and time – in place of war, out of the place of war, at a time of bombardment/closure/curfew, in a time of ceasefire, etc. – impact on the types of performance that emerge. War is affected by complex temporal and spatial categories – post-war, pre-war, military zone, demilitarised zone, cleared area, uncleared area, no man's land – and these are used here to intersect with ways of thinking about performance practice. (pp. 21–22)

This approach is valuable because it teaches us to recognise that the kinds of performance response that are most likely, possible or desirable in contexts of war and violence will vary according to the particular and shifting nature of those contexts. Some performances offer political and social commentary on war and violence; some engage with a post-violence desire for reconciliation or justice, or address issues relating to trauma; other performances are aimed at giving voice to particular people or perspectives during or in the aftermath of a violent conflict. Theatre and performance are used in all these ways and more, but different sorts of focus need and respond to different points in time and space in relation to the violence itself. A reconciliation project is unlikely while fighting is ongoing, for example: Farber's work is characterised by its engagement with the aftermath of Apartheid, as South Africans tried to deal with and ultimately move on from that violent and oppressive time.

In the examples discussed so far, the acts of performance have generally taken place at a spatial and/or temporal distance from the actual violence with which they engaged. *Close the Concentration Camps*, *This Is Camp X-Ray*, *Blasted* and *Lemkin's House* were all variously exploring and drawing attention to violence taking place in locations other than the sites at which they were performed. In their different ways, *Mercury Fur* and *Saved* both represented violence perhaps more local to but largely hidden from or ignored by many of the spectators to whom the plays were presented. *He Left Quietly*, while retaining an immediate spatial connection to the violence of Apartheid through Kumalo's presence as actor and character, was characterised and contextualised by its temporal distance from that violence. It is important to recognise that in all these examples distance is a significant factor in determining the nature of both the performances and their receptions.

Theatre and performance also happen absolutely at the time and place of violence, but it is worth noting that, as

Thompson, Hughes and Balfour discuss, performances created 'under the bombs' are not necessarily drawn to depictions or analyses of violence like those I have focused on here. Under such circumstances it is perhaps unsurprising that theatre offers opportunities to imagine a non-violent life, to escape from the realities of danger, horror and terror into playful and imaginative explorations of fun, hope and beauty, and we should not lose track of the value of these aspects of performance. This book is not the place for a detailed analysis of these issues, but at the end of a discussion of the many ways in which violence can be displayed and represented in performance, and in which performance can be used to perpetuate ideologies and acts of violence, it is worth pausing to note this point, from *Performance in Place of War*:

> The importance of the refrain 'making something beautiful' is frequently affirmed as a kind of aesthetic antidote to war but also as a means to prove one's humanity or create normalcy. [...] 'Theatre to make one human or normal', while begging questions of definition, at least asserts that a context of war should not be considered 'normal' or 'human'. Such terms require explanation but they are in themselves a form of criticism of the situations in which people find themselves. We may not know or agree what beauty is but the demand for it makes a direct point about war's ugliness. (p. 69)

Whether we choose to represent violent acts or not, it seems to me that theatre's responsibility is to help deny violence the status of 'normal' and 'human'. This does not mean denying that violence happens, or that it is perpetuated by humans, or that for many people it is so pervasive as to constitute a norm. The depiction and contemplation of violence offer numerous ways to challenge or undermine its prevalence in the world.

I began this book with the assertion that theatrical representations of violence can be necessary and valuable, providing space and focus for the consideration of violence in the world. I have gone on to argue for a rigorously analytical approach to all such acts of representation, and a recognition that the impact and effects of theatrical violence can be traced not just to the actions being shown but also to the manner and context of the showing.

This book is part of a series that offers its readers toolkits for thinking and talking about theatre and performance. *Theatre & Violence* is an attempt to prompt questions and to enable readers to find their own way through the fiery debates about the depiction of violence and its relationship to violence in the world. I have been keen throughout to persuade you to consider violence in context rather than as an ingredient to be listed, but the process of writing to an upper limit of 20,000 words has meant that I have had to take examples out of context, to choose single moments from longer and more complex and more nuanced texts and performances to serve as examples of different contexts and different forms of violence. I have shown you ways of approaching and thinking about specific examples in the hope that you find my thoughts useful as you develop your own opinions.

As I write my conclusion, though, I must admit that my head is filled with many examples of violent and upsetting depictions, often outside their contexts. The images are powerful and resonant and deeply distressing. To think about and to analyse violence is not a neutral or an emotionally disengaged process. In my experience, and in the examples I have used here, writers and performance-makers do not engage in the study and depiction of violence because they *like* or *admire* violence, but because they profoundly dislike it and seek to contribute to the making of a more peaceful and less violent world.

further reading

Actual violence is a perennial concern for philosophers and theorists, so there is a lot of reading material to choose from. Michel Foucault's ideas have been hugely influential on this still-growing field and his *Discipline and Punish* (1975) is well worth reading. Similarly, Hannah Arendt's *On Violence* (1970) remains useful. Judith Butler's pair of books *Precarious Life* (2004) and *Frames of War* (2009) make important philosophical contributions, and Slavoj Žižek's *Violence* (2008) is another more recent exploration of the area.

Of the books by fight directors on stage combat I recommend J. Allen Suddeth's *Fight Directing for the Theatre* (1996) and William Hobbs' *Fight Direction for Stage and Screen* (1995), both of which offer useful context and discussion alongside their focus on technique. Nicholas Sammond's edited collection *Steel Chair to the Head* (2005) has much to offer as a precise and engaging analysis of American professional wrestling, while Sharon Mazer's ethnographic study *Professional Wrestling: Sport and Spectacle* (1998) is an extremely good critical introduction to this performance form. Re-enactment has received increased scholarly attention in recent years, particularly within Heritage and Museum Studies. Although it does not all explore combat specifically, there is plenty of useful material in Iain McCalman and Paul A. Pickering's collection *Historical Reenactment* (2010).

Media Studies has produced many works that engage with the media effects model. In addition to those directly cited in this book I recommend *Ill Effects: The Media/Violence Debate* (2001), edited by Martin Barker and Julian Petley, which is a good introduction to the range of current perspectives. In *Theatres of Human Sacrifice* (2005), Mark Pizzato offers a fascinating historical analysis of violence in performance that connects ancient rituals and theatres with violence in films and includes a useful discussion of *Natural Born Killers*.

Performance Studies is a rich field of enquiry. As a starting point I recommend the excellent collection *Violence Performed* (2009), edited by Patrick Anderson and Jisha Menon, which includes chapters on hunger strikes, the South African Truth and Reconciliation Commission, and the Abu Ghraib torture photographs, all of which have direct relevance to the arguments presented here. Anthony Kubiak's work is important in this connection (note the dates, though: his *Stages of Terror* was written in 1991, before the 9/11 attacks in the United States).

Finally, James Thompson, Jenny Hughes and Michael Balfour's *Performance in Place of War* (2009) is an invaluable work, as is Jenny Hughes' book *Performance in a Time of Terror* (2011). Both are highly recommended to those interested in pursuing connections between performance and violence.

Abramović, Marina. *Rhythm 0*. 1974. Museum of Modern Art, New York. Interview. *MoMA Multimedia*. 10 Dec. 2012. <http://www.moma.org/explore/multimedia/audios/190/1972>.

Anderson, Patrick, and Jisha Menon, eds. *Violence Performed: Local Roots and Global Routes of Conflict*. Basingstoke, UK: Palgrave Macmillan, 2009.

Arendt, Hannah. *On Violence*. Orlando, FL: Harcourt, 1970.

Barker, Martin, and Julian Petley, eds. *Ill Effects: The Media/Violence Debate*. 2nd ed. London: Routledge, 2001.

Birkenstein, Jeff, Anna Froula, and Karen Randell, eds. *Reframing 9/11: Film, Popular Culture and the 'War on Terror'*. New York: Continuum, 2010.

Bond, Edward. 'On Violence'. *Plays One*. London: Methuen, 1977. 9–17.

———. 'Saved'. 1965. *Plays One*. London: Methuen, 1977. 19–133.

Brenton, Howard. *The Romans in Britain*. London: Methuen, 1981.

Butler, Judith. *Excitable Speech: A Politics of the Performative*. New York: Routledge, 1997.

———. *Frames of War: When Is Life Grievable?* London: Verso, 2009.

———. *Precarious Life: The Powers of Mourning and Violence*. London: Verso, 2004.

Cavarero, Adriana. *Horrorism: Naming Contemporary Violence*. 2007. Trans. William McCuaig. New York: Columbia UP, 2009.

Coward, Noël. *Private Lives*. 1930. London: Methuen, 2000.

Crouch, Tim. *The Author*. London: Oberon, 2009.

Das, Veena, Arthur Kleinman, Mamphela Ramphele, and Pamela Reynolds, eds. *Violence and Subjectivity*. Berkeley: U of California P, 2000.

Eagleton, Terry. *Marxism and Literary Criticism*. London: Routledge, 1976.

Farber, Yael. *Theatre as Witness: Three Testimonial Plays from South Africa.* London: Oberon, 2008.

Filloux, Catherine. 'Lemkin's House'. 2006. *Silence of God and Other Plays.* London: Seagull, 2009. 10–51.

Fitzpatrick, Lisa. 'The Performance of Violence and the Ethics of Spectatorship'. *Performance Research* 16.1 (2011): 59–67.

Foucault, Michel. *Discipline and Punish: The Birth of the Prison.* 1975. Trans. Alan Sheridan. London: Penguin, 1977.

Hand, Richard J., and Michael Wilson. *Grand-Guignol: The French Theatre of Horror.* Exeter: U of Exeter P, 2002.

Harpin, Anna. 'Intolerable Acts'. *Performance Research* 16.1 (2011): 102–11.

Harries, Martin. *Forgetting Lot's Wife: On Destructive Spectatorship.* New York: Fordham UP, 2007.

Hazou, Rand. 'Dys-appearance and Compassion: The Body, Pain and Ethical Enactments in Mike Parr's *Close the Concentration Camps* (2002)'. *Performing Ethos* 1.2 (2010): 153–67.

Herbert, Ian, and Kalina Stefanova, eds. *Theatre and Humanism in a World of Violence.* Sofia: St Kliment Ohridski UP, 2009.

Hobbs, William. *Fight Direction for Stage and Screen.* London: A&C Black, 1995.

Hughes, Jenny. *Performance in a Time of Terror: Critical Mimesis and the Age of Uncertainty.* Manchester: Manchester UP, 2011.

———. 'Theatre, Performance and the "War on Terror": Ethical and Political Questions Arising from British Theatrical Responses to War and Terrorism'. *Contemporary Theatre Review* 17.2 (2007): 149–64.

Jones, Amelia. *Body Art/Performing the Subject.* Minneapolis: U of Minnesota P, 1998.

Jones, Gerard. *Killing Monsters: Why Children Need Fantasy, Super Heroes, and Make-Believe Violence.* New York: Basic Books, 2002.

Kane, Sarah. *Blasted & Phaedra's Love.* London: Methuen, 1996.

Kubiak, Anthony. *Agitated States: Performance in the American Theater of Cruelty.* Ann Arbor: U of Michigan P, 2002.

———. *Stages of Terror: Terrorism, Ideology, and Coercion as Theatre History.* Bloomington: Indiana UP, 1991.

Level, Maurice. 'The Final Kiss' [*Le Baiser dans la nuit*]. 1912. Trans. Richard J. Hand and Michael Wilson. *Grand-Guignol: The French Theatre of Horror.* Exeter: U of Exeter P, 2002. 180–94.

Low, Jennifer A. *Manhood and the Duel: Masculinity in Early Modern Drama and Culture*. Basingstoke, UK: Palgrave Macmillan, 2003.

Mazer, Sharon. *Professional Wrestling: Sport and Spectacle*. Jackson: UP of Mississippi, 1998.

McCalman, Iain, and Paul A. Pickering, eds. *Historical Reenactment: From Realism to the Affective Turn*. Basingstoke, UK: Palgrave Macmillan, 2010.

Natural Born Killers. 1994. Dir. Oliver Stone. Perf. Woody Harrelson, Juliette Lewis. Warner Home Video, 2001. DVD.

Pizzato, Mark. *Theatres of Human Sacrifice: From Ancient Ritual to Screen Violence*. Albany: SUNY P, 2005.

Ridley, Philip. 'Mercury Fur'. 2005. *Plays 2*. London: Methuen, 2009. 71–202.

Ridley, Philip, and Aleks Sierz. '"Putting a New Lens on the World": The Art of Theatrical Alchemy'. *New Theatre Quarterly* 25 (2009): 109–17.

Sammond, Nicholas, ed. *Steel Chair to the Head: The Pleasure and Pain of Professional Wrestling*. Durham, NC: Duke UP, 2005.

Scarry, Elaine. *The Body in Pain: The Making and Unmaking of the World*. Oxford: Oxford UP, 1985.

Scott, John. *Power*. Cambridge: Polity, 2001.

Shakespeare, William. *King Henry IV, Part I*. Ed. David Scott Kastan. New ed. London: Bloomsbury, 2002.

————. *Romeo and Juliet*. Ed. G. Blakemore Evans. Cambridge: Cambridge UP, 2003.

Sontag, Susan. *Regarding the Pain of Others*. London: Penguin, 2003.

Suddeth, J. Allen. *Fight Directing for the Theatre*. Portsmouth, NH: Heinemann, 1996.

Thompson, James, Jenny Hughes, and Michael Balfour. *Performance in Place of War*. London: Seagull, 2009.

Trend, David. *The Myth of Media Violence*. Oxford: Blackwell, 2007.

White, Martin. *Renaissance Drama in Action: An Introduction to Aspects of Theatre Practice and Performance*. London: Routledge, 1998.

Žižek, Slavoj. *Violence: Six Sideways Reflections*. London: Profile, 2008.

index

acknowledgements

M y thanks go to Jenni Burnell, Jen Harvie and Dan Rebellato for their encouragement and their helpful comments on various drafts of this book.

This book is dedicated to Colette Conroy, whose enthusiasm, generosity and knowledge have elevated it and me at every stage.

Printed in China